Essential COOKING SERIES

COMPREHENSIVE, STEP BY STEP COOKING

Vegetarian Dishes

**BUDGET
BOOKS**

Food Editor: Jody Vassallo
Project Editor: Lara Morcombe
Design: Studio Pazzo
Cover Design: Budget Books

Essential Cooking Series: Vegetarian Dishes
This edition first published in 2008 by Budget Books
45–55 Fairchild Street
Heatherton, Victoria, 3202, Australia
www.hinklerbooks.com

10 9
13 12 11 10 09

Disclaimer: The nutritional information listed under each recipe does not
include the nutrient content of garnishes or any accompaniments not
listed in specific quantitites in the ingredient list. The nutritional
information for each recipe is an estimate only, and may vary depending on
the brand of ingredients used, and due to natural biological variations in
the composition of natural foods such as meat, fish, fruit and vegetables.
The nutritional information was calculated by using Foodworks dietary
analysis software (Version 3, Xyris Software Pty Ltd, Highgate Hill,
Queensland, Australia) based on the Australian food composition tables
and food manufacturers' data. Where not specified, ingredients are always
analysed as average or medium, not small or large.

ISBN: 978 1 7412 1945 6

Printed and bound in China

Contents

An introduction to vegetarian dishes

Short of curing cancer and promising never-ending longevity, vegetables are accredited with so many health benefits it's a wonder that their daily consumption is not a common obsession. Rich in vitamins, minerals and dietary fibre, vegetables are THE cornerstone of a healthy diet. Once the exclusive domain of vegetarians, vegetable-only meals are being incorporated into a growing number of weekly menu plans. And why not? They're good for your health, they help with weight loss and they're easy on the budget.

With increased demand comes increased availability and today's supermarkets and grocers offer an exciting diversity of vegetables. If you're shopping for lettuce, what type? Good shops will have at least 5 varieties on hand. Check out the cos, iceberg, mignonette, green coral, red coral, butter, endive, rocket and radicchio. And potatoes? Look for the pink eye, desiree, pontiac, king edward , new and sebago. Capsicums are available in a multitude of colours. Asian vegetables such as bok choy, chinese cabbage and ginger are plentiful and fresh.

The recipes in this book showcase the versatility of vegetables. Bolt down a quick snack of grilled vegetable bruschetta. Enjoy the lively taste of a tomato, mustard and brie tart. Or savour the flavours of a harvest vegetable bake. With this book on hand, vegetarian cooking need never be bland again.

BUYING AND STORING

When shopping for vegetables, it's worth remembering that freshness is important. Buy only what you need – shopping for small amounts of vegetables a few times a week is much better than a once weekly shop for everything. Plan meals with vegetables in season. These will be the freshest and most reasonably priced vegetables available. Watch the weather – long periods of rain can reduce the supply and the price will rise. If you establish a good relationship with your fruit and vegetable provider, they will be able to assist you in the best buys from week to week.

Also keep in mind that frozen vegetables can be added to soups and simmering dishes. Despite being frozen, they still contain nutrients and can be extremely handy if you don't have the time to shop every couple of days.

Lettuce and leafy greens

Look for lettuces and leafy greens with crisp shiny leaves. The base of the lettuce should be dry and not slimy. Wash the lettuce, remove the core and, if possible, spin dry in a

salad spinner or pat dry in a tea towel. Store the lettuce in a plastic bag or wrap in wetted absorbent paper in the crisper section of your refrigerator. Lettuce should keep for up to 7 days for the crisper varieties, softer leaf types will only last for 3–4 days. Salad leaves deteriorate after a few days, so it's best to only buy what you need; some supermarkets are now selling prepackaged salad mixes that last up to 5 days in the refrigerator.

Root vegetables

Avoid root vegetables with blemished skin, green or purple marks, a musty smell or that have started to sprout. Carrots, potatoes, parsnips, pumpkin, sweet potatoes, beetroots, celeriac, swedes, jerusalem artichokes and turnips are all quick to show signs of spoilage. When purchased, carrots should be firm with no sign of wrinkles. Store most root vegetables in the vegetable crisper of your refrigerator for 6–8 days.

There are many different varieties of potatoes available for cooking; the two main groups being floury and waxy. Floury potatoes are suited to baking, mashing and frying while waxy potatoes are good for boiling. Potatoes should be bought with the dirt still on to protect them from bruising and exposure to light. If stored in a cool dark place in a hessian bag, potatoes can last for up to 1 month.

Whole pumpkins will keep for months in a cool dark place. Wedges wrapped in plastic can be refrigerated for up to 3 days. Unless you have a good, sharp and large knife, it is probably best to buy pumpkin by the wedge. Check that the seed area is moist, but not slimy, and that there is no mould.

Tomatoes

Store tomatoes at room temperature as refrigerating will soften the flesh. To ripen tomatoes leave them on a window sill in a sunny spot in the kitchen. Unfortunately, the colour of a tomato is no longer indicative of the flavour. Vine ripened tomatoes that have been, as the name implies, left to ripen on the vine usually have a stronger sweeter flavour. Roma or egg tomatoes can also be sweet.

Brassicas

Cabbage, broccoli, cauliflower and brussels sprouts are quick to show signs of spoilage. With broccoli and cauliflower, look for tightly packed florets that show no evidence of yellowing or tiny flowers. Cabbages and brussels sprouts should be dense with crisp outer leaves.

Onions

Purchase onions with skins intact and no soft spots, green sprouts or any signs of moisture. Spring onions (also known as green onions) should have crisp green stems with moist roots.

Peas and beans

The best way to test the freshness of a bean is to bend it – if it snaps it is fresh, if it bends it is on its way out. Try to purchase beans loose as this allows you to pick your own. Store them in a plastic bag in your refrigerator for 2–3 days. Sugar snap and snow peas (also known as mangetout) should be crisp and bright green with no sign of blemishes; they should be eaten on the day of purchase. Buy peas in the pod and shell them just before cooking – 1 kg (2 lb) peas will yield 500 g (1 lb) shelled peas. About the only way to tell the sweetness of a pea is to put it to the taste test.

Capsicum

Look for capsicums (also known as peppers) with shiny waxy skins; they should also be heavy for their size with no signs of softening. They can be stored at room temperature for 1–2 days or in the vegetable crisper of the refrigerator for 4–5 days.

Celery, fennel and asparagus

Stalky vegetables should be crisp with upright stalks. Celery should have bright green leaves. Look for asparagus with firmly closed buds. Store stalky vegetables in the vegetable crisper for 2–3 days.

Avocado

To select a ripe avocado, gently press your thumb into the top near the stem and if it gives slightly it's ready to eat. Ripe ones should be eaten within 2–3 days of purchasing. Store unripe avocados at room temperature.

Sweet corn

Corn is best purchased in its husk. Peel back the husk and silk and check the kernels for signs of drying. Also, the silk should not be starting to moisten – the whiter the silk the fresher the corn. Corn is best eaten soon after purchase.

Mushrooms

Look for clean white mushrooms with a fresh earthy aroma and tight caps. Exotic mushrooms are usually sold in trays covered in plastic so check carefully for any signs of decay. Mushrooms last longer when stored in paper bags in the vegetable crisper in the refrigerator. Do not wash or peel mushrooms; brush clean with a piece of absorbent paper towel.

Spring vegetables

artichoke
asian greens
asparagus
avocado
beans
broccoli
cabbage
carrot
choko
cauliflower
cucumber
garlic
ginger
leek
lettuce
mushroom
onion
peas
pumpkin
silverbeet
spinach
sweet corn
watercress
zucchini flower

Summer vegetables

asparagus
avocado
beans
capsicum
celery
chilli
choko
cucumber
daikon
eggplant
lettuce
okra
onion
peas
radish
squash
sweet corn
tomato
watercress
zucchini
zucchini flower

Autumn vegetables

asian greens
avocado
beans
beetroot
broccoli
brussels sprouts
cabbage
capsicum
carrot
cauliflower
celery
chilli
cucumber
daikon
eggplant
fennel
garlic
ginger
leek
lettuce
mushroom
okra
olive
onion
parsnip
peas
potato
pumpkin
shallot
silverbeet
spinach
squash
swede
sweet potato
tomato
turnip
zucchini

Winter vegetables

asian greens
avocado
beetroot
broccoli
brussel sprouts
cabbage
carrot
cauliflower
celeriac
celery
fennel
garlic
ginger
horseradish
jerusalem artichoke
kale
kohlrabi
leek
okra
olive
onion
parsnip
pea
potato
pumpkin
shallot
silverbeet
spinach
swede
sweet potato
turnip
witlof

Grilled vegetable bruschetta

INGREDIENTS

1 red or yellow capsicum (pepper), sliced
1 zucchini (courgette), thinly sliced
1 red onion, thinly sliced
2 large plum tomatoes, thickly sliced
3 tablespoons extra virgin olive oil
2 tablespoons wholegrain mustard
black pepper
1 ciabatta loaf or baguette, cut into 8
  slices
1 clove garlic, halved
8 pitted black olives, thinly sliced
fresh basil to garnish

serves 4

PREPARATION TIME
15 minutes

COOKING TIME
20 minutes

1 Preheat grill to high and line with foil. Place capsicum, zucchini,
   onion and tomatoes in a bowl. In a small bowl whisk together 2
   tablespoons of oil, the mustard and black pepper, pour over
   vegetables and toss gently to coat.

2 Spread vegetables onto grill rack and grill for 3–4 minutes on each
   side, until lightly browned. Set aside and keep warm.

3 Toast bread on both sides and rub garlic halves over one side.
   Divide the vegetables between the toast slices, garlic side up. Top
   with remaining olives and drizzle with remaining oil. Garnish with
   basil and serve

NUTRITIONAL VALUE PER SERVE   FAT 1 G   CARBOHYDRATE 1.8 G   PROTEIN 7 G

Artichokes with soured cream sauce

INGREDIENTS

4 large globe artichokes
280 ml (9 fl oz) sour cream
5 spring onions (green onions), finely chopped
1 tablespoon balsamic vinegar
1 clove garlic, finely chopped
serves 4

PREPARATION TIME
10 minutes

COOKING TIME
50 minutes, plus 30 minutes standing

1 Cut off artichoke stalks, so artichokes stand flat. Place in a large pan of boiling water and simmer, partly covered, for 40 minutes or until tender. To test if artichokes are cooked, pull off an outside leaf – it should come away easily. Remove from pan and set aside for 30 minutes to cool.

2 In a large bowl combine sour cream, spring onions, vinegar and garlic. Pull central cone of leaves out of each artichoke, leaving leaves around the edge, and discard. Scrape away the inedible core to leave the edible base.

3 Spoon sauce into artichoke centre. Place artichokes on plates and eat by plucking out a leaf and dipping it into the sauce. Use your teeth to pull away the edible fleshy part at the base of the leaf, then discard the rest.

NUTRITIONAL VALUE PER SERVE	FAT 10 G	CARBOHYDRATE 1.6 G	PROTEIN 1.9 G

Watercress roulade with parmesan

INGREDIENTS

oil for greasing
2 tablespoons parmesan, grated
90 g (3 oz) watercress, finely
  chopped (thick stems discarded)
4 eggs, beaten
salt and black pepper
filling
210 g (7 oz) cream cheese,
  at room temperature
3 tablespoons milk
90 g (3 oz) watercress, finely chopped
  (thick stems discarded)
5 spring onions (green onions),
  finely chopped
extra watercress sprigs to garnish
serves 4

PREPARATION TIME
15 minutes

COOKING TIME
1 hour 15 minutes

1 Preheat oven to 200°C (400°F, gas mark 6). Grease a 23 x 30 cm Swiss roll tin, line with baking paper, sprinkle with 1 tablespoon of parmesan.

2 Mix together the watercress and eggs, season and pour into tin. Cook for 7–8 minutes, until the eggs have set. Remove from oven and leave to cool for 5 minutes. Sprinkle with remaining parmesan. Lay a sheet of baking paper over the top and set aside until cool.

3 Combine cream cheese, milk, watercress, onions and seasoning. Turn roulade onto a chopping board. Peel baking paper off the base and spread filling over the base. Roll up from the short end, discarding any paper as you go. Refrigerate for 30 minutes, and serve in slices, garnished with watercress.

NUTRITIONAL VALUE PER SERVE   FAT 13.8 G   CARBOHYDRATE 1.2 G   PROTEIN 8.8 G

Ricotta herb dip with garlic toasts

INGREDIENTS

6 pitted green olives, finely chopped
1 tablespoon chopped fresh tarragon
1 tablespoon chopped fresh chives
1 tablespoon chopped fresh mint
2 teaspoons finely grated lemon rind
  (zest)
250 g (8 oz) ricotta cheese
black pepper
4 tablespoons sun-dried tomato
  purée
1 large mixed grain baguette, cut into
  thick slices
1 clove garlic, halved
serves 4

PREPARATION TIME
10 minutes

COOKING TIME
10 minutes

1 In a large bowl combine olives, tarragon, chives, mint and lemon rind, and stir in ricotta. Season with pepper, mix well. Add sun-dried tomato purée and stir gently to create a marbled effect. Spoon into a serving dish.

2 Preheat grill to high. Grill baguette slices for 1–2 minutes on each side, until golden. Rub garlic halves over toast slices and serve with ricotta dip.

NUTRITIONAL VALUE PER SERVE   FAT 4.3 G   CARBOHYDRATE 38 G   PROTEIN 8.5 G

Mixed mushrooms on herbed muffins

INGREDIENTS

500 g (1 lb) mixed mushrooms,
   including wild, oyster and shiitake
2 tablespoons olive oil
salt and black pepper
2 tablespoons butter
1 clove garlic, crushed
3 tablespoons chopped fresh parsley
3 tablespoons finely snipped chives
extra chives for garnish
2 teaspoons balsamic vinegar
4 tablespoons soft cheese
6 white muffins
serves 6

PREPARATION TIME
15 minutes

COOKING TIME
15 minutes

1 Halve any large mushrooms. Heat 2 teaspoons of oil in a large frying pan, add mushrooms, season lightly and cook over a medium-high heat for 5 minutes, until moistened.

2 Remove mushrooms, drain on kitchen towels and set aside. Add remaining oil and half the butter to the pan and heat until butter melts. Add garlic and cook for 1 minute.

3 Return mushrooms to the pan, increase heat to high and fry for 5 minutes, until tender and starting to crisp. Stir in remaining butter and 2 tablespoons each of parsley and chives. Drizzle with vinegar and season.

4 Mix soft cheese with remaining parsley and chives. Split and toast the muffins. Spread cheese mixture over the muffin halves. Top with mushrooms and garnish with chives.

NUTRITIONAL VALUE PER SERVE   FAT **9.5** G   CARBOHYDRATE **14.1** G   PROTEIN **6.6** G

Mixed bean and vegetable soup

INGREDIENTS

110 g (3$\frac{1}{2}$ oz) dried haricot beans,
   soaked overnight
110 g (3$\frac{1}{2}$ oz) dried chickpeas, soaked
   overnight
3 tablespoons olive oil
1 onion, chopped
1 clove garlic, crushed
1 leek (white part only), diced
1.5 litres (2$\frac{1}{2}$ pints) vegetable stock
2 sticks celery, sliced
1 carrot, diced
2 sprigs fresh thyme, chopped
1 small fennel bulb, grated
2 zucchini (courgettes), grated
90 g (3 oz) broad beans
3 tomatoes, peeled, deseeded and
   chopped
salt and freshly ground black pepper
grated parmesan, to serve
serves 4–6

PREPARATION TIME
30 minutes, plus
overnight soaking

COOKING TIME
1 hour 50 minutes

1 Drain the haricot beans and chickpeas. Place in a large pan, cover with water and bring to the
   boil for 15 minutes. Reduce heat, cover and simmer for a further 30 minutes. Drain well.

2 Heat oil in a large pan, add onion, garlic and leek. Cook on a medium-high heat, stirring,
   until tender. Add stock, haricot beans and chickpeas. Reduce heat, cover and simmer for 45
   minutes until tender. Add remaining ingredients and simmer for a further 15 minutes.

3 Season to taste. Serve with grated parmesan.

NUTRITIONAL VALUE PER SERVE	FAT 2.1 G	CARBOHYDRATE 2.6 G	PROTEIN 1.7 G

Pea and fresh mint soup

INGREDIENTS

4 tablespoons butter
1 bunch spring onions (green onions),
   chopped
500 g (1 lb) peas
2 little gem lettuces, shredded
salt and black pepper
2 tablespoons chopped fresh mint
900 ml (1 ½ pints) water
155 ml (5 fl oz) cream
salt and black pepper
pinch of castor sugar (optional)
lemon juice (optional)
extra cream to serve
fresh chives, snipped to garnish
serves 4

PREPARATION TIME
15 minutes

COOKING TIME
30 minutes

1 Melt butter in a large pan, add spring onions, cover, reduce heat and cook gently
   for 5 minutes, stirring occasionally, until onions have softened.

2 Add peas, lettuce, mint and water. Bring to the boil, reduce heat and simmer for
   10 minutes, until vegetables are tender. Cool. In a food processor, combine pea
   mixture and cream until smooth.

3 Return soup to the pan. Season to taste, add castor sugar and lemon juice, if
   using. Reheat gently – do not allow soup to boil. Serve in bowls drizzled with
   cream and garnished with chives.

NUTRITIONAL VALUE PER SERVE	FAT 5.5 G	CARBOHYDRATE 2.5 G	PROTEIN 2.4 G

Spinach and nutmeg soup with cheese toasts

INGREDIENTS

2 tablespoons olive oil
2 tablespoons butter
250 g (8 oz) floury potatoes, cut
  into chunks
250 g (8 oz) spinach leaves
1 teaspoon freshly grated nutmeg
salt and black pepper
1.4 litres (2½ pints) chicken or
  vegetable stock
4 tablespoons crème fraîche
100 g (3½ oz) gruyère, grated
1 large egg, beaten
day-old narrow french bread stick,
  cut diagonally into 18 x 1 cm
  slices
serves 6

1 Heat oil and half the butter in a large pan. Fry potatoes for 1 minute, add spinach and nutmeg. Cook for 2 minutes, until spinach is wilting.

2 Add stock, season lightly and bring to the boil. Reduce heat, cover and simmer for 10–15 minutes, until potatoes are tender. Leave to cool for 10 minutes.

3 In a food processor, combine until smooth. Stir in half the crème fraîche, season to taste and set aside.

4 Preheat grill. Mix grated cheese, egg and remaining crème fraîche. Lightly toast the bread, spread cheese mixture on one side of each slice. Dot with remaining butter and season with black pepper. Grill for 5 minutes, until bubbling and golden. Return soup to pan and heat gently. Serve topped with cheese toasts.

PREPARATION TIME
25 minutes

COOKING TIME
35 minutes

| NUTRITIONAL VALUE PER SERVE | FAT 6.4 G | CARBOHYDRATE 11.3 G | PROTEIN 5.6 G |

Coconut, sweet potato and spinach soup

INGREDIENTS

2 tablespoons butter
500 g (1 lb) sweet potatoes, diced
1 onion, chopped
2 cloves garlic, crushed
1 teaspoon grated ginger
1 tablespoon medium curry paste
600 ml (1 pint) vegetable stock
220 ml (7$^{1}/_{2}$ fl oz) coconut milk
juice of 1 lime
$^{1}/_{4}$ teaspoon dried crushed chillies
185 g (6 oz) spinach, shredded
salt and black pepper
serves 4

1 Melt butter in a large pan, fry potatoes, onion, garlic, ginger and curry paste on a medium-high heat for 5 minutes until lightly golden.

2 Add stock, coconut milk, lime juice and chilli. Bring to the boil, reduce heat, cover and simmer for 15 minutes, until potatoes are tender.

3 Remove from heat and set aside to cool. In a food processor, purée half the soup. Return purée to the pan, stir to combine, add spinach and cook for 1–2 minutes, until spinach has just wilted and soup has heated through. Season to taste.

PREPARATION TIME
20 minutes

COOKING TIME
30 minutes

NUTRITIONAL VALUE PER SERVE	FAT **5.1** G	CARBOHYDRATE **5.1** G	PROTEIN **1.7** G

Carrot and lentil soup

INGREDIENTS

2 tablespoons butter
1 tablespoon sunflower oil
500 g (1 lb) carrots, chopped
1 onion, chopped
2 celery sticks, chopped
100 g (3½ oz) red split lentils, rinsed
850 ml (1½ pints) vegetable stock
sea salt and freshly ground black
  pepper
natural yoghurt
fresh parsley, chopped to garnish
serves 4

PREPARATION TIME
20 minutes

COOKING TIME
40 minutes

1 Melt butter and oil in a large pan. Fry carrots, onion and celery for
  6–8 minutes until lightly golden. Add lentils and 750 ml (1¼ pints)
  of vegetable stock, bring to the boil. Reduce heat, cover and
  simmer for about 20 minutes, until carrots are tender.

2 Allow soup to cool. In a food processor, combine until smooth.
  Return to a clean pan with remaining stock, season to taste and
  reheat gently before serving. Garnish with a swirl of yoghurt and
  chopped parsley.

NUTRITIONAL VALUE PER SERVE   FAT 3.4 G   CARBOHYDRATE 5.2 G   PROTEIN 2.4 G

Tomato and mozzarella

INGREDIENTS

6 plum tomatoes, sliced

250 g (8 oz) mozzarella, drained and
   sliced

2 spring onions (green onions), sliced

90 g (3 oz) black olives

salt and black pepper

dressing

3 tablespoons extra virgin olive oil

1 clove garlic, crushed

2 teaspoons balsamic vinegar

2 tablespoons chopped fresh basil

serves 4

PREPARATION TIME
10 minutes

COOKING TIME
15 minutes

1 Arrange tomatoes, mozzarella, spring onions and olives in layers
   on serving plates and season.

2 Heat oil and garlic in a small pan over a low heat for 2 minutes
   until garlic has softened. Remove from heat, add vinegar and
   basil, whisk to combine and pour over salad.

NUTRITIONAL VALUE PER SERVE   FAT 13.6 G   CARBOHYDRATE 3.5 G   PROTEIN 8.5 G

Roasted vegetable salad

INGREDIENTS

3 red onions, quartered
3 potatoes, cut into wedges
2 zucchini (courgettes), thickly sliced
2 yellow capsicums (peppers),
  thickly sliced
4 tomatoes, halved
2 tablespoons olive oil
sea salt and freshly ground black
  pepper
parmesan shavings (optional)
dressing
3 tablespoons extra virgin olive oil
2 tablespoons clear honey
1 tablespoon balsamic vinegar
juice and finely grated rind (zest) of
  $1/2$ lemon
serves 2–4

PREPARATION TIME
20 minutes

COOKING TIME
35 minutes

1 Preheat oven to 200°C (400°F, gas mark 6). Place all vegetables in a shallow roasting tin, drizzle with oil and season. Shake tray gently to coat vegetables. Bake for 35 minutes, until vegetables are tender and lightly browned.

2 In a small bowl combine all dressing ingredients. Pour over roasted vegetables, tossing gently to coat. Serve topped with parmesan shavings.

| NUTRITIONAL VALUE PER SERVE | FAT 4.7 G | CARBOHYDRATE 7.4 G | PROTEIN 1.3 G |

Zucchini and hazelnut salad

INGREDIENTS

650 g (1 lb 5 oz) small zucchini
  (courgettes)
2 tablespoons sunflower oil
extra sunflower oil for frying
$^1/_2$ cup (125 ml, 4 fl oz) walnut oil
1 tablespoon white-wine vinegar
salt and black pepper
100 g ($3^1/_2$ oz) whole blanched
  hazelnuts
170 g ($5^1/_2$ oz) watercress (thick stalks
  removed)
90 g (3 oz) feta, crumbled
serves 6

PREPARATION TIME
25 minutes

COOKING TIME
25 minutes

1 Pare zucchini into lengthways slivers, using a vegetable peeler. In a bowl, combine
   sunflower oil, walnut oil and vinegar, and season. Add half the zucchini slivers to the
   mixture, toss lightly and set aside.

2 Brush a large frying pan with a little sunflower oil and heat. Lay the remaining slivers in
   the pan and cook for 2 minutes on each side, until lightly charred. Remove, season and set
   aside. Wipe the pan clean.

3 Roughly crush hazelnuts, using a pestle and mortar. Place in the frying pan and cook for
   1–2 minutes, until golden.

4 Divide the watercress between serving plates. Spoon some of the marinated zucchini into
   the centre, reserving some of the marinade. Scatter over half the toasted hazelnuts and
   the feta. Arrange the charred zucchini on top, sprinkle over the rest of the hazelnuts and
   the reserved marinade.

| NUTRITIONAL VALUE PER SERVE | FAT **19.0** G | CARBOHYDRATE **1.4** G | PROTEIN **3.6** G |

Tomato, mustard and brie tart

INGREDIENTS

185 g (6 oz) plain white flour
pinch of sea salt
90 g (3 oz) butter, diced
1/2 cup (125 ml, 4 fl oz) milk
2 egg yolks
1 clove garlic, crushed
1 tablespoon wholegrain mustard
60 g (2 oz) mature cheddar, grated
4 tomatoes, sliced
125 g (4 oz) brie, thinly sliced
sea salt and freshly ground black pepper
herb oil
1 tablespoon finely chopped fresh basil
1 tablespoon finely chopped fresh parsley
1 tablespoon finely chopped fresh
   coriander
2 tablespoons extra virgin olive oil
serves 4

1 Preheat oven to 190°C (375°F, gas mark 5). Sift flour and a pinch of sea salt into a large bowl. Using your fingertips, rub butter into flour until it resembles fine breadcrumbs. Add 2 tablespoons of cold water and mix to dough. Cover and refrigerate for 20 minutes. Roll pastry to line a deep 20 cm metal flan tin. Chill for a further 10 minutes.

2 Line pastry with baking paper and baking beans, bake blind for 10–12 minutes. Carefully remove paper and beans. Bake pastry for a further 5 minutes and set aside. Reduce oven temperature to 180°C (350°F, gas mark 4).

3 In a jug, place milk, egg yolks, garlic and seasoning. Whisk to combine. Spread mustard over pastry base and sprinkle with cheddar. Arrange tomatoes and brie on top, pour over egg mixture. Cook for 30–35 minutes, until just set and golden. In a small bowl, combine remaining ingredients and drizzle over tart. Serve warm.

PREPARATION TIME
25 minutes

COOKING TIME
1 hour 30 minutes

NUTRITIONAL VALUE PER SERVE	FAT **2.2** G	CARBOHYDRATE **1.9** G	PROTEIN **11.5** G

Tortellini with tomato and cream sauce

INGREDIENTS

4 tablespoons butter
1 small onion, finely chopped
1 stick celery, finely chopped
400 g (13 oz) tomato paste
1/2 teaspoon castor sugar
155 ml (5 fl oz) crème fraîche
600 g (1 1/4 lb) fresh spinach and
  ricotta tortellini
salt and black pepper
parmesan, grated to serve
serves 4

PREPARATION TIME
15 minutes

COOKING TIME
45 minutes

1 Melt butter in a large pan. Add onion, celery, tomato paste and
   sugar, and bring to the boil. Reduce heat and simmer, uncovered,
   for 30 minutes or until sauce has thickened.

2 Spoon in crème fraîche, season and bring back to the boil, stirring.
   Simmer for 1 minute and season to taste.

3 Cook pasta in a large pan of boiling water until al dente. Drain
   well, transfer to a serving bowl and pour over sauce. Garnish with
   parmesan.

NUTRITIONAL VALUE PER SERVE	FAT 8 G	CARBOHYDRATE 4 G	PROTEIN 1.3 G

Harvest vegetable bake

INGREDIENTS

1 onion, sliced
2 leeks, sliced
2 sticks celery, chopped
2 carrots, thinly sliced
1 red capsicum (pepper), sliced
500 g (1 lb) mixed root vegetables
  (sweet potato, parsnip, turnip etc.),
  cubed
185 g (6 oz) mushrooms, sliced
400 g (13 oz) can tomatoes, chopped
$^1/_2$ cup (125 ml, 4 fl oz) dry cider
1 teaspoon dried thyme
1 teaspoon dried oregano
black pepper
fresh herbs of choice to garnish
serves 4

PREPARATION TIME
30 minutes

COOKING TIME
1$^1/_2$ hours

1 Preheat oven to 180°C (350°F, gas mark 4). Place the onion, leeks, celery, carrots, capsicum, root vegetables and mushrooms in a large ovenproof casserole dish and mix well. Stir in the tomatoes, cider, thyme, oregano and black pepper.

2 Cover and bake in centre of oven for 1–1$^1/_2$ hours until the vegetables are cooked through and tender, stirring once or twice. Garnish with fresh herbs.

| NUTRITIONAL VALUE PER SERVE | FAT 0.5 G | CARBOHYDRATE 5.4 G | PROTEIN 1.5 G |

Mixed vegetable cheese bake

INGREDIENTS

1 large butternut pumpkin, cut
   into chunks
salt and black pepper
3 tablespoons olive oil
1 large (about 800 g, 1 lb 10 oz)
   cauliflower, cut into florets
360 g (12 oz) mushrooms, sliced
2 tablespoons fresh white breadcrumbs
2 tablespoons grated parmesan
sauce
2 tablespoons butter
30 g (1 oz) plain flour
pinch of cayenne pepper
300 ml (10 fl oz) milk
1 teaspoon English mustard
100 g (3 1/2 oz) cheddar, grated
extra butter for greasing
black pepper
serves 4

1 Preheat oven to 200°C (400°F, gas mark 6). Place
pumpkin into an ovenproof dish, season, drizzle
with half the oil. Roast for 25 minutes, stirring once,
until tender. Cook cauliflower in a large pan of
boiling water for 5 minutes, until just tender. Drain,
reserving 220 ml (7 1/2 fl oz) of the cooking water,
refresh in cold water and set aside. Heat remaining
oil in a large frying pan. Cook mushrooms on a
medium-high heat until just tender, tossing gently.

2 Melt butter in a large pan, stir in flour and cayenne
pepper. Cook on a medium low heat for 2 minutes,
gradually stir in reserved cooking liquid. Cook for
2–3 minutes, until thick, gradually stir in the milk.
Simmer, stirring, for 10 minutes. Remove from heat,
stir in mustard and cheese, until melted. Season to
taste.

3 Reduce oven temperature to 180°C (350°F, gas mark
4). Add cauliflower to pumpkin, toss gently to
combine. Divide between four individual ovenproof
dishes, top with mushrooms and pour over sauce.
Combine breadcrumbs and parmesan, and sprinkle
over each dish. Bake for 30–35 minutes.

PREPARATION TIME
30 minutes

COOKING TIME
1 hour 15 minutes

NUTRITIONAL VALUE PER SERVE	FAT 5.1 G	CARBOHYDRATE 4.3 G	PROTEIN 3.2 G

Pasta with double tomato sauce

INGREDIENTS

1 tablespoon extra virgin olive oil

1 red onion, finely chopped

2 celery sticks, finely chopped

400 g (13 oz) can tomatoes, chopped

1 tablespoon tomato purée

280 ml (9 fl oz) vegetable stock

250 g (8 oz) cherry tomatoes, halved

1 teaspoon brown sugar

340 g (11¼ oz) dried gemelli or
  penne

2 tablespoons crème fraîche

sea salt and freshly ground black
  pepper

serves 4

1 Heat oil in a large pan, add red onion and celery. Cook, uncovered, for 5 minutes on a medium heat, until vegetables are tender. Add chopped tomatoes, tomato purée and stock. Bring to the boil and simmer, uncovered, for 15 minutes, stirring occasionally until reduced and thickened.

2 Add cherry tomatoes, sugar and season to taste. Stir gently for about 3 minutes until heated through. Cook pasta in a large pan of boiling water until al dente, and drain. Pour the sauce over the pasta, toss gently to combine and serve topped with crème fraîche.

PREPARATION TIME
20 minutes

COOKING TIME
35 minutes

NUTRITIONAL VALUE PER SERVE   FAT 2 G   CARBOHYDRATE 2.4 G   PROTEIN 0.8 G

Linguine with leeks and mushrooms

INGREDIENTS

500 g (1 lb) leeks, sliced
290 g (10 oz) button mushrooms, sliced
1 bay leaf
3 tablespoons butter
45 g (1½ oz) plain flour
2 cups (500 ml, 16 fl oz) low-fat milk
2 tablespoons snipped fresh chives
extra chives to garnish
black pepper
500 g (1 lb) fresh linguine or tagliatelle
serves 4

1 Steam leeks, mushrooms and bay leaf over a large pan of boiling water for 10–15 minutes until tender. Discard bay leaf and keep vegetables warm.

2 Melt butter in a large pan, add flour and cook gently for 1 minute, stirring. Remove from heat and gradually add milk. Return to heat and bring to the boil, stirring, until thickened. Reduce heat and simmer for 2 minutes, stirring. Add leek and mushrooms, chives and black pepper, heat through.

3 Cook pasta in a large pan of boiling water until al dente. Drain well, return to pan, add leek and mushroom sauce and toss lightly to combine. Garnish with fresh chives.

PREPARATION TIME
20 minutes

COOKING TIME
30 minutes

NUTRITIONAL VALUE PER SERVE   FAT **3** G   CARBOHYDRATE **23** G   PROTEIN **5.9** G

Rich bean and vegetable stew

INGREDIENTS

125 g (4 oz) dried porcini mushrooms
3 tablespoons olive oil
250 g (8 oz) large mushrooms, chopped
2 carrots, finely diced
1 large potato, diced
250 g (8 oz) baby beans, chopped
$^1/_2$ tablespoon dried thyme
$^1/_2$ tablespoon dried sage
2 cloves garlic, crushed
300 ml (10 fl oz) red wine
$2^1/_2$ cups, (600 ml, 1 pint) vegetable stock
250 g (8 oz) broad beans
300 g (10 oz) can cannellini beans
225 g ($7^1/_2$ oz) can flageolet beans
salt and black pepper
serves 4

PREPARATION TIME
30 minutes

COOKING TIME
1 hour

1 Cover porcini mushrooms with $2^1/_2$ cups (600 ml, 1 pint) of boiling water, soak for 20 minutes. Heat oil in a large pan, add fresh mushrooms, carrots, potato and green beans. Fry gently for 3–4 minutes, until slightly softened.

2 Add thyme, sage and garlic, the porcini mushrooms and liquid, the red wine, stock and seasoning. Bring to the boil, reduce heat and simmer, uncovered, for 20 minutes, until vegetables are tender.

3 Add broad beans, simmer for a further 10 minutes until tender. Drain and rinse the cannellini and flageolet beans, add to mixture, stir to combine. Simmer for 2–3 minutes, until heated through.

NUTRITIONAL VALUE PER SERVE	FAT 2.3 G	CARBOHYDRATE 5.1 G	PROTEIN 3.5 G

Asparagus, ricotta and herb frittata

INGREDIENTS

500 g (1 lb) fresh asparagus
12 eggs
2 cloves garlic, crushed
4 tablespoons chopped fresh
  mixed herbs (basil, chives,
  parsley etc.)
salt and black pepper
4 tablespoons butter
100 g (3½ oz) ricotta
squeeze of lemon juice
olive or truffle oil to drizzle
parmesan to serve
extra whole chives to garnish
serves 4

1 Preheat grill to high. Char grill asparagus on a griddle pan, until browned. Set aside and keep warm.

2 In a large bowl, whisk together eggs, garlic, herbs and seasoning. Melt half of the butter in an ovenproof frying pan, immediately pour in a quarter of the egg mixture and cook for 1–2 minutes, until almost set.

3 Place under preheated grill for 3–4 minutes, until egg is cooked through and top of frittata is set, transfer to a plate. Keep warm whilst making remaining frittatas, adding more butter when necessary.

4 Place frittatas on 4 serving plates and arrange a quarter of asparagus and a quarter of ricotta over each frittata. Squeeze over lemon juice, season and drizzle with oil. Top with shavings of parmesan and garnish with fresh chives.

PREPARATION TIME
20 minutes

COOKING TIME
30–35 minutes

NUTRITIONAL VALUE PER SERVE   FAT **10** G   CARBOHYDRATE **0.8** G   PROTEIN **8** G

Sweet potato puree

INGREDIENTS

750 g (1 ½ lb) sweet potatoes,
  cut into large chunks
3 tablespoons milk
1 clove garlic, crushed
45 g (1 ½ oz) mature cheddar,
  finely grated
1 tablespoon chopped fresh parsley
1 tablespoon snipped fresh chives
black pepper
extra chives to garnish
serves 4

1 Cook sweet potatoes in a large pan of boiling water for 10–15 minutes, until tender. Drain thoroughly, mash until smooth.

2 Heat milk in a small pan, add to potato along with garlic, cheddar, parsley, chives and black pepper. Beat until smooth and well combined. Serve garnished with fresh chives.

PREPARATION TIME
10 minutes

COOKING TIME
20 minutes

| NUTRITIONAL VALUE PER SERVE | FAT 2 G | CARBOHYDRATE **11.7** G | PROTEIN **3.5** G |

Sweet and sour red cabbage

INGREDIENTS

3 tablespoons olive oil
2 tablespoons red-wine vinegar
1 red or green chilli, sliced, seeds
   and pith included
grated rind (zest) and juice of
   1 orange
1 tablespoon orange-flower water
3 tablespoons light muscovado
   sugar
1 red cabbage, thinly sliced
serves 4

1 Preheat oven to 160°C (315°F, gas mark 3). Place oil, vinegar, chilli, orange rind and juice, orange-flower water and sugar into a small pan, bring to the boil, reduce heat and simmer for 5 minutes.

2 Place cabbage in an ovenproof casserole dish, pour over oil and vinegar mixture, reserving about 2 tablespoons. Cover and bake for 3 hours, until cooked through. Toss with reserved oil and vinegar mixture.

PREPARATION TIME
20 minutes

COOKING TIME
3 hours

NUTRITIONAL VALUE PER SERVE   FAT 6.2 G   CARBOHYDRATE 8.6 G   PROTEIN 1.4 G

Green beans with walnut dressing

INGREDIENTS

450 g (14 oz) green beans
2 tablespoons walnut oil
1 tablespoon olive oil
1 tablespoon white-wine vinegar
1 teaspoon dijon mustard
black pepper
serves 4

PREPARATION TIME
10 minutes

COOKING TIME
15 minutes

1 Cook beans in a large pan of boiling water for 5–6 minutes until tender.

2 Place walnut oil, olive oil, vinegar, mustard and black pepper in a small bowl, whisk to combine. Drain the beans and serve hot or cold drizzled with dressing.

NUTRITIONAL VALUE PER SERVE	FAT **7.2** G	CARBOHYDRATE **1.9** G	PROTEIN **1.9** G

Snowpeas and carrots with sesame seeds

INGREDIENTS

$^1/_2$ cucumber
2 tablespoons sesame seeds
1 tablespoon sunflower oil
4 carrots, julienned
250 g (8 oz) snow peas (mangetout)
6 spring onions (green onions),
  chopped
1 tablespoon lemon juice
black pepper
serves 4

PREPARATION TIME
20 minutes

COOKING TIME
20 minutes

1 Peel cucumber, cut in half lengthways and scoop out seeds. Slice into half moons.

2 Heat a non-stick wok or large frying pan. Add sesame seeds and dry-fry on a
  medium heat for 1 minute until toasted, tossing constantly. Remove and set aside.
  Add oil and heat. Add cucumber and carrots, and stir-fry over a high heat for
  2 minutes. Add snowpeas and spring onions and stir-fry for a further 2–3 minutes,
  until vegetables are tender but crunchy.

3 Add lemon juice and sesame seeds, toss gently to combine. Season with pepper
  and serve.

NUTRITIONAL VALUE PER SERVE	FAT 3.5 G	CARBOHYDRATE 4.5 G	PROTEIN 1.8 G

Asparagus with lemon sauce

INGREDIENTS

2 bunches (about 500 g, 1 lb)
  asparagus
salt and black pepper
sauce
2 eggs
2 tablespoons chopped pickled
  cucumber
1 teaspoon chopped capers
1 teaspoon dijon mustard
¹/₂ cup (125 ml, 4 fl oz) olive oil
finely grated rind (zest) and juice of
  ¹/₂ lemon
pinch of castor sugar (optional)
2 tablespoons chopped fresh parsley
2 tablespoons crème fraîche
serves 4

1 Place eggs in a small pan of cold water, bring to the boil and cook for 10 minutes. Run under cold water, peel, halve and remove yolks, discarding the whites.

2 In a food processor combine yolks, pickled cucumber, capers, mustard and gradually add oil until well combined. Add lemon rind, juice and sugar, if using. Process until combined. Stir in parsley and crème fraîche, and set aside.

3 Cut ends off asparagus, peel the lower half using a vegetable peeler to expose flesh. Fill a large pan with about 4 cm water, bring to the boil. Stand asparagus spears in the pan, keeping tips out of the water. Reduce heat and simmer for 5–6 minutes, until just tender, drain. Serve asparagus topped with sauce and season with black pepper.

PREPARATION TIME
20 minutes

COOKING TIME
20 minutes

| NUTRITIONAL VALUE PER SERVE | FAT **16.5** G | CARBOHYDRATE **1.9** G | PROTEIN **3.2** G |

Potato and onion dauphinoise

INGREDIENTS

1 tablespoon butter

extra butter for greasing

750 g (1½ lb) baking potatoes, thinly sliced

3 onions, thinly sliced

1 teaspoon freshly grated nutmeg

450 ml (14 fl oz) cream

salt and black pepper

serves 2–4

1 Preheat oven to 180°C (350°F, gas mark 4). Grease a shallow ovenproof dish with butter.

2 Arrange potatoes and onions in alternate layers in baking dish. Lightly season each layer with salt, pepper and nutmeg. Finish with a potato layer, pour over cream and dot with butter. Place on lower shelf of oven and cook for 1 hour until golden.

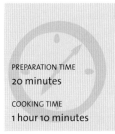

PREPARATION TIME
20 minutes

COOKING TIME
1 hour 10 minutes

NUTRITIONAL VALUE PER SERVE	FAT **14.1** G	CARBOHYDRATE **8.5** G	PROTEIN **2** G

Zucchini polenta slices

INGREDIENTS

1 tablespoon butter
extra butter for greasing
3 tablespoons olive oil
250 g (8 oz) zucchini (courgettes),
  grated
3 cups, 750 ml (1¼ pints) chicken or
  vegetable stock
185 g (6 oz) instant polenta
salt and black pepper
2 tablespoons grated parmesan
serves 4

PREPARATION TIME
15 minutes

COOKING TIME
20 minutes

1 Grease a shallow 22 cm square roasting tin. Heat the butter and 1 tablespoon of oil in a large frying pan. Fry zucchini on a medium heat for 3–4 minutes, until softened but not browned, stirring frequently. Remove from heat and set aside.

2 Bring stock to the boil in a large pan. Sprinkle in polenta, stirring with a wooden spoon, and continue to stir for 5 minutes, until polenta thickens and begins to come away from the sides of the pan. Remove from the heat and stir in zucchini. Season to taste.

3 Turn polenta mix into the roasting tin, spreading evenly, sprinkle with parmesan and leave for 1 hour to cool and set.

4 Heat a ridged cast-iron grill pan over a high heat. Cut polenta into slices, brush with remaining oil and cook for 2–4 minutes on each side, until golden.

NUTRITIONAL VALUE PER SERVE	FAT 6.3 G	CARBOHYDRATE 10.5 G	PROTEIN 2.4 G

Glossary

Al dente: Italian term to describe pasta and rice that are cooked until tender but still firm to the bite.

Bake blind: to bake pastry cases without their fillings. Line the raw pastry case with greaseproof paper and fill with raw rice or dried beans to prevent collapsed sides and puffed base. Remove paper and fill 5 minutes before completion of cooking time.

Baste: to spoon hot cooking liquid over food at intervals during cooking to moisten and flavour it.

Beat: to make a mixture smooth with rapid and regular motions using a spatula, wire whisk or electric mixer; to make a mixture light and smooth by enclosing air.

Beurre manié: equal quantities of butter and flour mixed together to a smooth paste and stirred bit by bit into a soup, stew or sauce while on the heat to thicken. Stop adding when desired thickness results.

Bind: to add egg or a thick sauce to hold ingredients together when cooked.

Blanch: to plunge some foods into boiling water for less than a minute and immediately plunge into iced water. This is to brighten the colour of some vegetables; to remove skin from tomatoes and nuts.

Blend: to mix 2 or more ingredients thoroughly together; do not confuse with blending in an electric blender.

Boil: to cook in a liquid brought to boiling point and kept there.

Boiling point: when bubbles rise continually and break over the entire surface of the liquid, reaching a temperature of 100°C (212°F). In some cases food is held at this high temperature for a few seconds then heat is turned to low for slower cooking. See simmer.

Bouquet garni: a bundle of several herbs tied together with string for easy removal, placed into pots of stock, soups and stews for flavour. A few sprigs of fresh thyme, parsley and bay leaf are used. Can be purchased in sachet form for convenience.

Caramelise: to heat sugar in a heavy-based pan until it liquefies and develops a caramel colour. Vegetables such as blanched carrots and sautéed onions may be sprinkled with sugar and caramelised.

Chill: to place in the refrigerator or stir over ice until cold.

Clarify: to make a liquid clear by removing sediments and impurities. To melt fat and remove any sediment.

Coat: to dust or roll food items in flour to cover the surface before the food is cooked. Also, to coat in flour, egg and breadcrumbs.

Cool: to stand at room temperature until some or all heat is removed, e.g. cool a little, cool completely.

Cream: to make creamy and fluffy by working the mixture with the back of a wooden spoon, usually refers to creaming butter and sugar or margarine. May also be creamed with an electric mixer.

Croutons: small cubes of bread, toasted or fried, used as an addition to salads or as a garnish to soups and stews.

Crudite: raw vegetable sticks served with a dipping sauce.

Crumb: to coat foods in flour, egg and breadcrumbs to form a protective coating for foods which are fried. Also adds flavour, texture and enhances appearance.

Cube: to cut into small pieces with six even sides, e.g. cubes of meat.

Cut in: to combine fat and flour using 2 knives scissor fashion or with a pastry blender, to make pastry.

Deglaze: to dissolve dried out cooking juices left on the base and sides of a roasting dish or frying pan. Add a little water, wine or stock, scrape and stir over heat until dissolved. Resulting liquid is used to make a flavoursome gravy or added to a sauce or casserole.

Degrease: to skim fat from the surface of cooking liquids, e.g. stocks, soups, casseroles.

Dice: to cut into small cubes.

Dredge: to heavily coat with icing sugar, sugar, flour or cornflour.

Dressing: a mixture added to completed dishes to add moisture and flavour, e.g. salads, cooked vegetables.

Drizzle: to pour in a fine thread-like stream moving over a surface.

Egg wash: beaten egg with milk or water used to brush over pastry, bread dough or biscuits to give a sheen and golden brown colour.

Essence: a strong flavouring liquid, usually made by distillation. Only a few drops are needed to flavour.

Fillet: a piece of prime meat, fish or poultry which is boneless or has all bones removed.

Flake: to separate cooked fish into flakes, removing any bones and skin, using 2 forks.

Flame: to ignite warmed alcohol over food or to pour into a pan with food, ignite then serve.

Flute: to make decorative indentations around the pastry rim before baking.

Fold in: combining of a light, whisked or creamed mixture with other ingredients. Add a portion of the other ingredients at a time and mix using a gentle circular motion, over and under the mixture so that air will not be lost. Use a silver spoon or spatula.

Glaze: to brush or coat food with a liquid that will give the finished product a glossy appearance, and on baked products, a golden brown colour.

Grease: to rub the surface of a metal or heatproof dish with oil or fat, to prevent the food from sticking.

Herbed butter: softened butter mixed with finely chopped fresh herbs and re-chilled. Used to serve on grilled meats and fish.

Hors D'Oeuvre: small savoury foods served as an appetiser, popularly known today as 'finger food'.

Infuse: to steep foods in a liquid until the liquid absorbs their flavour.

Joint: to cut poultry and game into serving pieces by dividing at the joint.

Julienne: to cut some food, e.g. vegetables and processed meats into fine strips the length of matchsticks. Used for inclusion in salads or as a garnish to cooked dishes.

Knead: to work a yeast dough in a pressing, stretching and folding motion with the heel of the hand until smooth and elastic to develop the gluten strands. Non-yeast doughs should be lightly and quickly handled as gluten development is not desired.

Line: to cover the inside of a baking tin with paper for the easy removal of the cooked product from the baking tin.

Macerate: to stand fruit in a syrup, liqueur or spirit to give added flavour.

Marinade: a flavoured liquid, into which food is placed for some time to give it flavour and to tenderise. Marinades include an acid ingredient such as vinegar or wine, oil and seasonings.

Mask: to evenly cover cooked food portions with a sauce, mayonnaise or savoury jelly.

Pan-fry: to fry foods in a small amount of fat or oil, sufficient to coat the base of the pan.

Parboil: to boil until partially cooked. The food is then finished by some other method.

Pare: to peel the skin from vegetables and fruit. Peel is the popular term but pare is the name given to the knife used; paring knife.

Pith: the white lining between the rind and flesh of oranges, grapefruit and lemons.

Pit: to remove stones or seeds from olives, cherries, dates.

Pitted: the olives, cherries, dates etc, with the stone removed, e.g. purchase pitted dates.

Poach: to simmer gently in enough hot liquid to almost cover the food so shape will be retained.

Pound: to flatten meats with a meat mallet; to reduce to a paste or small particles with a mortar and pestle.

Simmer: to cook in liquid just below boiling point at about 96°C (205°F) with small bubbles rising gently to the surface.

Skim: to remove fat or froth from the surface of simmering food.

Stock: the liquid produced when meat, poultry, fish or vegetables have been simmered in water to extract the flavour. Used as a base for soups, sauces, casseroles etc. Convenience stock products are available.

Sweat: to cook sliced onions or vegetables, in a small amount of butter in a covered pan over low heat, to soften them and release flavour without colouring.

Conversions

Measurements differ from country to country, so it's important to understand what the differences are. This Measurements Guide gives you simple 'at-a-glance' information for using the recipes in this book, wherever you may be.

Cooking is not an exact science – minor variations in measurements won't make a difference to your cooking.

EQUIPMENT

There is a difference in the size of measuring cups used internationally, but the difference is minimal (only 2–3 teaspoons). We use the Australian standard metric measurements in our recipes:

1 teaspoon ....5 ml	1 tablespoon....20 ml
¹/₂ cup......125 ml	1 cup.....250 ml
4 cups...1 litre	

Measuring cups come in sets of one cup (250 ml), ¹/₂ cup (125 ml), ¹/₃ cup (80 ml) and ¹/₄ cup (60 ml). Use these for measuring liquids and certain dry ingredients.

Measuring spoons come in a set of four and should be used for measuring dry and liquid ingredients.

When using cup or spoon measures always make them level (unless the recipe indicates otherwise).

DRY VERSUS WET INGREDIENTS

While this system of measures is consistent for liquids, it's more difficult to quantify dry ingredients. For instance, one level cup equals: 200 g of brown sugar; 210 g of castor sugar; and 110 g of icing sugar.

When measuring dry ingredients such as flour, don't push the flour down or shake it into the cup. It is best just to spoon the flour in until it reaches the desired amount. When measuring liquids use a clear vessel indicating metric levels.

Always use medium eggs (55–60 g) when eggs are required in a recipe.

OVEN

Your oven should always be at the right temperature before placing the food in it to be cooked. Note that if your oven doesn't have a fan you may need to cook food for a little longer.

MICROWAVE

It is difficult to give an exact cooking time for microwave cooking. It is best to watch what you are cooking closely to monitor its progress.

STANDING TIME

Many foods continue to cook when you take them out of the oven or microwave. If a recipe states that the food needs to 'stand' after cooking, be sure not to overcook the dish.

CAN SIZES

The can sizes available in your supermarket or grocery store may not be the same as specified in the recipe. Don't worry if there is a small variation in size – it's unlikely to make a difference to the end result.

dry		liquids	
metric (grams)	imperial (ounces)	metric (millilitres)	imperial (fluid ounces)
		30 ml	1 fl oz
30 g	1 oz	60 ml	2 fl oz
60 g	2 oz	90 ml	3 fl oz
90 g	3 oz	100 ml	3 1/2 fl oz
100 g	3 1/2 oz	125 ml	4 fl oz
125 g	4 oz	150 ml	5 fl oz
150 g	5 oz	190 ml	6 fl oz
185 g	6 oz	250 ml	8 fl oz
200 g	7 oz	300 ml	10 fl oz
250 g	8 oz	500 ml	16 fl oz
280 g	9 oz	600 ml	20 fl oz (1 pint)*
315 g	10 oz	1000 ml (1 litre)	32 fl oz
330 g	11 oz		
370 g	12 oz		
400 g	13 oz		
440 g	14 oz		
470 g	15 oz		
500 g	16 oz (1 lb)		
750 g	24 oz (1 1/2 lb)		
1000 g (1 kg)	32 oz (2 lb)		*Note: an American pint is 16 fl oz.

cooking temperatures	°C (celsius)	°F (fahrenheit)	gas mark
very slow	120	250	1/2
slow	150	300	2
moderately slow	160	315	2–3
moderate	180	350	4
moderate hot	190	375	5
	200	400	6
hot	220	425	7
very hot	230	450	8
	240	475	9
	250	500	10

Index

Essential COOKING SERIES

COMPREHENSIVE, STEP BY STEP COOKING

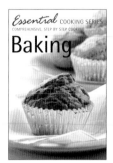

Essential COOKING SERIES
COMPREHENSIVE, STEP BY STEP COOKING
Baking

Essential COOKING SERIES
COMPREHENSIVE, STEP BY STEP COOKING
Chicken Meals

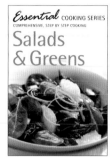

Essential COOKING SERIES
COMPREHENSIVE, STEP BY STEP COOKING
Salads & Greens

Essential COOKING SERIES
COMPREHENSIVE, STEP BY STEP COOKING
Soups & Hors D'Oeuvres

Essential COOKING SERIES
COMPREHENSIVE, STEP BY STEP COOKING
Meat Dishes

Essential COOKING SERIES
COMPREHENSIVE, STEP BY STEP COOKING
Finger Food

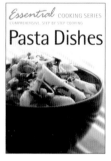

Essential COOKING SERIES
COMPREHENSIVE, STEP BY STEP COOKING
Pasta Dishes

Essential COOKING SERIES
COMPREHENSIVE, STEP BY STEP COOKING
Grilling & Barbecuing

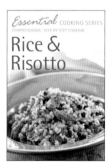

Essential COOKING SERIES
COMPREHENSIVE, STEP BY STEP COOKING
Rice & Risotto

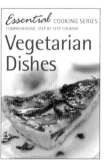

Essential COOKING SERIES
COMPREHENSIVE, STEP BY STEP COOKING
Vegetarian Dishes

Essential COOKING SERIES
COMPREHENSIVE, STEP BY STEP COOKING
Asian Dishes

Essential COOKING SERIES
COMPREHENSIVE, STEP BY STEP COOKING
Stir-Fry